Crescendo Publishing Presents

Instant Insights on...

WELLNESS

Career Wellness *for* Chronic Illness Warriors

Diana Hallare, MPH, CWWS

small guides. BIG IMPACT.

Instant Insights on...
Career Wellness for Chronic Illness Warriors
By Diana Hallare

Crescendo Publishing, LLC
300 Carlsbad Village Drive
Ste. 108A, #443
Carlsbad, California 92008-2999

www.CrescendoPublishing.com
GetPublished@CrescendoPublishing.com
1-877-575-8814

ISBN: 978-1-944177-89-8 (P)
ISBN: 978-1-944177-90-4 (E)

Printed in the United States of America
Cover design by Melody Hunter

10 9 8 7 6 5 4 3 2 1

What You Will Learn in This Book

Do you want meaningful work? Do you feel that your health is stopping you?

You are not alone if you want work to give you a sense of mission and fulfillment. You are not alone if your wellbeing is not as optimal as you want it to be. You are not alone if you wish for improvement in your career, your health, and your life.

This is the only self-help wellness + career book meant for individuals who are living with chronic health conditions, which can strike anyone regardless of age or race. Chronic health conditions are long-term diseases or disorders, and they can cause disability.

Career Wellness for Chronic Illness Warriors navigates you through common problems via practical solutions and straightforward tips. Wherever in the career path you happen to be – job searching, building a startup business, or "stable" in a job – this book will help you thrive. This book is also packed with inspirational anecdotes, uplifting personal stories, motivational quotes, and questions for reflection. You will find simple yet powerful examples and advice for self-care and career-building. You will gain new perspectives through exposure to multiple distinctive work philosophies.

If you have fears about health and work, this book will help you manage both your chronic condition(s) and your career, empowering you to evolve with more confidence, optimism, and direction. In short, you will find no better tool to help you champion your health, your rights, and your happiness through work that you love.

You'll get *Instant Insights* on...

- Building an awesome resume

- Overcoming stigma, broken dreams, and workplace bullies

- Working with accommodations

- Stress management and productivity at work

- Loving your work

A Gift from the Author

To help you implement the strategies mentioned in this *Instant Insights™* book and get the most value from the content, the author has prepared the following bonus materials we know you will love:

- The Progress Zone, a mini monthly planner

You can get instant access to these complimentary bonus materials here:
http://www.chroniconomics.com

Dedication

To the people who never give up advocating for themselves and others.

Table of Contents

Finding Sustainability 1

The Stigma Dilemma 9

Broken Dreams 15

Finding Opportunities.. 21

Finding More Knowledge 29

Getting Accommodations.. 35

Worsening Health... 41

Losing Productivity 47

Handling Stress.. 53

Workplace Bullies 59

Loving Your Work... 65

About the Author 71

Connect with the Author.. 73

Acknowledgements.. 75

Resources 77

References.. 79

About Crescendo Publishing.. 85

Finding Sustainability

Learn your way to success.

"Learning is the beginning of health," Jim Rohn – an author, motivational speaker, and entrepreneur – said.

Do you feel you want to give up your job search after the application process has drained your energy at the end of the day? Or are you searching for another job to keep you afloat while you struggle to pay for medical bills, loans, and other expenses? Are you so worried and stressed out about making ends meet that you are worsening your health?

If you struggle to be sustainable, healthy, and independent, remember that your set of footprints may be similar to someone else's, but never identical. Your DNA and its manifestation are unique, and so is your destiny. Keep moving forward even if you do not emulate others' successes. Your terms of success are defined by your vision, your attitude, and your impact. But they are also defined by your circumstances – such as your health.

Living with one or more chronic conditions is already a challenge. Chronic conditions can be a cause of disability, which can hamper a person's career. According to the Bureau of Labor Statistics, only 17.9% of people living with a disability were employed in 2016. Among these workers, 34% were employed only part-time.

I have lived with my health issue for years, which broke my dreams and sometimes lowered my self-esteem. Envy and self-pity crept in. I asked myself, "How did others succeed ahead of me when they partied harder?" The shame and desperation for financial independence triggered cycles of illness.

However, over time, I found three *ships* that took me on a journey to find sustainability. They helped me discover my passions and dislikes, identify my strengths and weaknesses, and utilize my experiences in order to improve my spirits as well as my resume. Technically, at least three means of sustainability exist: working in a job, running a business, and a combination of both. But the three *ships* I mentioned provided further clarity.

The first *ship* is community service leadership. I delivered presentations on behalf of nonprofit organizations. I volunteered to teach crafts and creative writing to people living with disabilities. I organized art shows, which honed my teamwork, event management, and design skills. These activities gave me a sense of hope and a feeling of accomplishment.

The second *ship* is internship. I worked as an intern with and without pay. I became familiar with the careers and operational practices of many different institutions, from the university science lab to the public health agency. I experienced a sense of self-worth and practiced collaboration, asking questions, and speaking up.

The third *ship* is entrepreneurship. I started businesses, which sometimes ended sooner than planned. However, I grew in creativity and built skill sets in terms of networking, creating web sites, and marketing.

Several common threads exist among the three *ships*. First, I was willing to learn. Second, I was determined to thrive. Third, I did not give up. I took joy in my post-college career(s), from teaching to writing to promoting health. I am still enjoying my job as a health education specialist, a position that allows me to combine most of my talents, passions, skills, and knowledge to create a positive impact on the community. I am also happy to embrace and cultivate the other side of me: a side that strives to empower people who are living with chronic conditions and/or disabilities.

Do you have to experience all three *ships* as I did? The solution to sustainability and a career you love is to enrich your experience first. This would enhance your resume, your interview answers, and your outlook on life, career, and the world.

How can you go through the three *ships* if you have a chronic condition and/or disability? One way is to use technology. For example, you can be a remote intern via the Internet, using email and other forms of digital communication. You can start, promote, and manage a social media forum that would gather and engage people who share the same chronic condition(s). You can sell virtual and physical products through e-commerce.

Nevertheless, chronic conditions fall along a spectrum: mild (and/or completely invisible) to severe (and/or completely noticeable). Don't let your chronic conditions stop you, wherever you lie along this spectrum.

It does not matter how old you may be when chronic illness strikes. Chronic illness does not mean defeat. I once heard a health professional say: Everyone goes through a chronic health condition from some point in life; the difference is how people deal with that illness. Chronic conditions change lives, yet they can provide inspiration. If you show hope and optimism, you will have better chances of lightening up the world around you and strengthening the best in you.

Some people make their condition the very point around which their career evolves and revolves. For example, disability advocates, Nick Vujicic and Jessica Cox often speak to the public about the adversities that they face being born without limbs. Their career successes reflect how they live their life to the fullest: they never stop giving, learning, or believing. They touch upon other topics too, such as bullying, spirituality, and leadership. Better yet, they reflect on these experiences on a positive note, even with humor.

Other people make their condition a more silent part of their public life. This is also a valid approach. Consider Franklin D. Roosevelt's story: he was stricken with the poliovirus in his late thirties. He became paralyzed for the rest of his life; he could no longer walk. At the time of his diagnosis, he was running for one of the top political seats in the land. Therefore, at first, he did not expose his disability. Yet it was this hardship that allowed him to face other challenges, especially rising to meet the challenges of the Great Depression and World War II during his presidency. He became an icon of greatness despite, and because he triumphed over, the flaws in his health.

No matter how you treat or disclose your chronic condition, choose to live. Choose to hope. Choose to love who you are and what you do so that you will build your self-confidence. Choose to learn, and make those lessons work for you. No matter which *ship* you choose, sail away to sustainability. Be proactive, and start as early as possible. Start now.

Your Instant Insights...

- Build your resume through experiential learning opportunities: volunteering, internships, and entrepreneurship. Act upon your lessons.

- You can build your career around your health condition or you can choose not to focus on your chronic illness/disability.

- Live and work with hope.

The Stigma Dilemma

Stigma is the shame you and/or others impose upon you.

It is often associated with health issues, such as AIDS and mental illness.

Brené Brown, a sociologist and expert on the topic of vulnerability said, "Shame needs three things to grow exponentially: secrecy, silence, and judgment."

Have you ever kept your chronic condition(s) a secret out of fear and shame? And if you did mention your health issues, have you ever suffered discrimination or even lost friends?

I did. It hurt.

Disclosure must be based upon your discretion and your particular comfort level.

Not everyone in the world welcomes every story. Though it feels liberating to voice our individual stories, it is best to be wise.

A common question in job applications and interviews, as well as on college and scholarship applications, is "Describe a hardship and how you overcame it." You do not need to divulge too much personal information: parenting, marital or relationship status, family life, and so on. In a similar vein, you do not need to mention your health condition(s), unless the job or scholarship description specifically calls for it. For example, a Peer Support Specialist position in the mental health field may require experience living with a mental health issue in order to find compassionate and knowledgeable mental health caregivers. Similarly, a scholarship for cancer survivors must confirm that applicants have indeed suffered from cancer.

Certain laws in the United States specifically protect the rights of individuals with health conditions. The Equal Employment Opportunity Act prohibits discrimination against people with disabilities. The Americans with Disabilities Act gives similar protection. The Health Insurance Portability and Accountability Act helps to keep your health information private and secure.

So empower yourself, and do not fear.

Indeed, health issues can be a foundation for building resilience...but how?

First, socialize without the pressure to disclose your health issues. If someone asks you, "How are you?" you do not need to give a list of personal complaints. Be positive, and speak with gratitude. Answering the question – if you prefer not to say the ordinary "I'm fine, thank you," – could be "I'm grateful for..." Fill in the blank. You can talk about the accomplishment you had for the day, or even the weather and why.

Gratitude helps reduce the stigma and self-pity. According to Psychology Today contributor Amy Morin, benefits of gratitude include the following:

1. more relationships and more opportunities
2. better physical and emotional health, more happiness
3. more empathy
4. better sleep
5. better self-esteem
6. reduced stress and reduced impact from trauma

When you socialize, smile. The joyful face is not merely a façade, but can be a mark of resilience and strength. It is about celebrating life despite challenges.

Where can you socialize? Various groups are available according to interest. If you are intent on self-development, try the local Toastmasters club. If you would like to grow in spirituality and/or service, join a church ministry. If you would like a community through which you can learn more about your health, find a shoulder (or a few) to cry on, and/or celebrate the small and big positive things in your life, feel free to confide in a support group.

Building resilience requires specific dreams, specific visions, and specific goals. So the second way to build resilience is to let your pain – physical and/or emotional – fuel your determination to succeed. Let your condition inspire you, and you will inspire others too.

Cliff Scherb is a triathlon athlete with diabetes. He keeps track of how much sugar is in his blood, how many carbohydrates he eats, how long/strenuously he exercises, and how fast his heart beats. He figured out the exact ratios that he needs to endure each race. Despite failing in a few Ironman races, he worked hard and triumphed as a 6-time USAT All American triathlete. He is also an entrepreneur who coaches other athletes, some of whom have diabetes as well.

I have known parents who shield their kids with chronic illness from society. This is not healthy. For me, knowing I have a health condition makes me more determined to manage it while showing the world that I will not give up and that I am still rising.

I have made friends who also endure chronic conditions, but whose faith is strengthened and dreams are fortified because of their health.

Take care of yourself...not only your physical and emotional self, but also the part of you that wants to touch other people's lives and leave a legacy. Fear is not a suitable legacy, but overcoming fear through courage and perseverance are virtues to be cherished and celebrated.

So say goodbye to stigma. It is not always easy, but you can do it.

Your Instant Insights...

- You don't need to disclose your chronic condition(s)/disability to everyone, such as at interviews.

- Socialize without the pressure to disclose. Socialize with gratitude.

- Pursue your dreams and make your health issue an inspiration.

Broken Dreams

One source of health-related stigma is broken dreams.

Almost 40% of students with disabilities do not graduate from high school in the United States. This can mean many lost opportunities and many broken dreams.

Have you ever experienced a broken heart because of a broken dream? Did you blame yourself and/or someone else for the "failure?" Did you express anger, cry, or isolate yourself?

For a few years, every March to June, I cringed inside as I scrolled through social media. This period was graduation time in both the Philippines and the United States. On the outside, I seemed happy to already hold an advanced degree. But inside, I struggled to understand my identity, especially after a variety of rejections and failed attempts.

I am glad and grateful about where I am now. I have been healing to the point where I celebrate others' successes from the heart, without comparisons, and without the negativity.

Les Brown, a motivational speaker said, "You are never too old to set another goal or to dream a new dream."

That was what I did: I dreamed new and bigger dreams that fit my values, and I set new goals. One of my values has been personal wellness: self-care as a top priority.

My current job allows me to continue learning and to accomplish much along the way. Achievements such as earning new certifications and co-organizing conferences were dreams once upon a time, and I am overjoyed to realize them.

A big dream does not always equate to a big bank account or investment portfolio. It may not always result in prestige or fame.

To dream big may mean making a substantial impact on the community, even at the local level. It may mean a personal change, such as a miraculous recovery or the elimination of a bad habit. Dreams are as unique as the individual imaginations of those who dream them. Someone may inspire you, but you do not always need to be a copycat. Embrace common threads, but follow your own path.

So if any of your dreams are broken, two options exist: continue your pursuit of the old dream (even if you require *traffic diversion*) or pursue a new dream.

Kadeena Cox is an athlete whose dream was to compete as a sprinter in the Olympics. However, a few years before the big event, she was diagnosed with multiple sclerosis, a nervous system disorder that affects her mobility. She did not give up and entered the 2016 Paralympics in Rio. She won two Paralympic gold medals – one for parasprinting and one for paracycling – establishing new world records in each event.

This is an example of a *traffic diversion*, or a new route, as well as a *dream modification.* The path to the goal/dream may not always be straight or fast. It is not about settling for less. It is about accepting different ways to fulfill your potential.

Many people talk about Plan B. However, the best plan is Plan BE. This is to BE who you are and the best person you are meant to BE.

The emotional pain of bearing dreams broken by transitions in health can teach many lessons and help individuals to become stronger. Carrying this pain as emotional baggage for too long, however, can take a toll on mental health, which in turn can worsen physical health in a vicious cycle. Depression, for example, is known to suppress the immune system, which weakens the body's defenses against infection and illness.

So take up something new or polish an already existing passion, talent, or craft. Build your career around this new or renewed dream.

If job applications do not work out, explore entrepreneurship. If entrepreneurship does not work out, go (back) to the job search. If you want to juggle both a job and a business, the combination is worth considering.

But listen to your heart and your body, not just your mind. If you are already too tired from work and if adding something to your plate would harm your health, you may need to re-assess your situation. Avoid burnout, or at least recognize the early warning signs and fix the problem as best as you can. Prioritize your values. Learn when to say no.

When you dream again and anew, you may have a million ideas. That is all right; you are practicing creativity. Not all ideas are viable. Some ideas may be interconnected. But you must learn when to let go of some ideas just as you must learn to let go of the hurt from an old and unrealized dream.

You may be desperate to heal completely at once. Understand that healing takes time, a supportive environment, and a supportive self.

Keep moving on, moving forward. Keep dreaming and goal-setting. Even when you achieve your dream, go back to the drawing board. You can dream anew. You can dream again.

Your Instant Insights...

- With broken dreams, either go another route to achieve the renewed dream or completely change course with another dream.

- Do not forget self-care.

- Learn to let go. Follow the plan of fulfilling your own potential, which does not always mean copying others' dreams.

Finding Opportunities

Opportunities do not hide.

When you seek them, keep your eyes and ears open.

Could your chronic condition be an opportunity for something better? Is it a new call for self-care, a new/different career, a need for more family time, or a decision to pursue your lifelong dreams and passions?

Kobe Bryant, a retired professional basketball player said, "Everything negative – pressure, challenges – is all an opportunity for me to rise."

Again, I emphasize learning, socializing, and networking. Today, these types of opportunities abound.

You can attend a brick-and-mortar college, adult school, or community center to learn skills that interest you, be they speaking conversational Spanish or taking professional-level photography. You can also take online courses that can help you delve into computer coding or update your marketing know-how. Tuition-free programs like MissionU and the Holberton School equip youth with the skills and experience that are required in many of today's jobs.

You can listen to podcasts and webinars, read blogs and books, or watch videos and professionals in action. You can also find a career mentor and/or coach.

To make more connections, you can attend speed networking sessions, meet-ups, business groups, job fairs, and conferences according to your interests. Let your budget of money and time determine the number of groups or events that you find worthy.

Understand what you can do and what you want to do. Research each group/event and the opportunities that it presents. For example, if you are a nurse looking for a job or graduate school opportunity, why not go to nursing or healthcare conferences? You can check out the booths at the trade show or expo. By contrast, it might not make sense to fly across the nation for a writers' conference unless you also have a writing gig on the side.

Other opportunities to learn and connect include involvement in community service, volunteer mission trips, and business incubators or leadership cultivators.

No matter what opportunity you choose to pursue, take the lead. Be the first to greet. Take the initiative to build a team. Take the guts to delegate. Take the courage to ask. Take the opportunity to grow.

Rejections may still come. I have faced them from employers, literary agents, graduate schools, a millennial talent/leadership incubator, writing contests, singing auditions, and so on.

But as my high school friend once said: NO only means "Next Opportunity."

I love the two mantras from entrepreneur James Altucher:

1. Grow yourself 1% every day. (Now if only this were applicable to height, I would be eligible for the modeling industry – just kidding.)
2. Choose yourself.

Growing yourself involves learning, working hard to polish your craft/creativity, and making connections.

Why is it important to make connections? No matter if you are an introvert, an extrovert, or something in-between, you need social support for both health and career reasons. We all need cheerleaders, teammates, and companions in our journey.

It is healthy to talk and express yourself. Indeed, alone time can be refreshing, but too much isolation is a cause for concern.

Our careers revolve around people. Who are our customers? Who are our colleagues and supervisors? They are people. And you are a person too.

A quality connection can help you get a job, secure a promotion, or take advantage of a business opportunity. Friends on social media do not necessarily provide you with career stability. However, those who show care can often lend a hand...especially if you provide value to them and/or reciprocate their good deeds.

For example, a chosen few among my connections have recommended me through letters and social media. Through my current job experience, I am learning about building relationships with stakeholders. I have phoned, emailed, and visited key people in the community who can help me fulfill my professional role. They do not serve as mentors but as influencers to other people who make a difference in my field.

I enjoy my career. It is not helpful to call first contacts "cold" (*cold* calls, *cold* emails, *cold* visits). Rather, I would say they are *opportunity* calls/ emails/visits. I prepare for these opportunities by conducting my research, fine-tuning my proposals, and understanding how my agency and I can contribute.

At the same time, when building a career, it is important to have champions of support. For me, my champion network consisted of family, friends, my healthcare team, and local employment support agencies in both the government and the private sectors. They encouraged both the pursuit of an ideal career and the enhancement of my creativity.

I love my current job because of the flexibility, the degree of independence, the fast pace, the lack of monotony, and the contribution that I make to society. This was a perfect match for my skills and interests. I also fell in love with what I do because the people around me have been friendly, optimistic, and positive. I am glad I chose to say yes to this opportunity.

In choosing yourself, creativity is the cornerstone. James Altucher recommends writing a list of ten creative ideas each day to practice and grow creativity. If finding opportunity is a challenge, then create your own.

I have pursued entrepreneurship too and had fun. The thrill comes whenever someone purchases and praises your products and services. However, frustration sometimes sets in, so perseverance is key.

Open your eyes and reach out to grab the opportunities around you. At my job, I often get a chance to flex my creative muscles, and I take/create opportunities to spread a healthful message wherever I am. At church, I sing and read scripture. At an arts center, I teach creative writing (after approaching the programs director with a proposal for my class). In my business, I speak, write, create, and interact with people every day. I am blessed for these opportunities to develop who I am and what I do.

Collette Divitto is a woman with Down's syndrome – she loves baking. After several job rejections, she opened her own bakery, Collettey's. Receiving thousands of orders soon after her company's opening, she has become so successful that her story went viral online.

Do not be afraid to innovate. By making you stand out, innovation can ultimately make your dreams come true.

When opportunities come, sometimes they come in a flood. You possess the power to say yes or no to any of them.

Fall in love with who you are, with what you do, and with your biggest dreams. Find a way to connect with people and opportunities. Most of all, while you grow and create, stay true to yourself.

Your Instant Insights...

- Pursue educational and networking opportunities for personal development/ advancement.

- Get champions to support your endeavors.

- Innovate. Make and choose your own opportunities.

Finding More Knowledge

Searching for options often requires research.

The astronaut Neil Armstrong said, "Research is creating new knowledge."

Have you ever felt stuck, not knowing what to do? Have you ever experienced writer's block? A cure for this intangible barrier is research, and you don't need to have a doctorate to do it.

Creating new knowledge = Learning something new.

For my formal education, research was the core of many papers and projects. For my job search, I used search engines, LinkedIn, and networking opportunities to reach out to people who either were employers or had connections. In writing this book, research has also been a key.

When you research, you have an aim to answer specific questions.

When you live with a chronic condition and want to build your career, these are three questions you can keep in mind:

1. What career options – job/business opportunities – are open to/ideal for me?
2. What options for treatment and management do I have for my health?
3. What are my rights and responsibilities?

Researching these questions will make you aware of the possibilities and what they entail.

When you find information and/or answers, make sure that they are evidence-based. This means that the source of the information is credible and that the information is entirely factual.

The Internet is an enormous library. However, not everything online is true.

When you find a job opportunity, make sure it is with a real company and not a scam. Check the profile of each company online... its official website, LinkedIn page, Glassdoor reviews, and more as available. Read the job description and highlight the skills and accomplishments on your resume that match the qualifications of the job.

When you find a certain treatment for your condition(s), figure out the advantages and disadvantages. Weigh the pros and cons of factors such as location and potential costs. Does the healthcare provider hold a medical license and training in that specialty? What is the provider's overall reputation?

For health information, you can check reputable, credible websites - such as WebMD, the Mayo Clinic, or the Cleveland Clinic - which offer simple explanations with a minimum of jargon. If you want more detailed information, you can check the Cochrane reviews or research databases such as PubMed and Google Scholar.

You can benefit from knowing the laws that provide protection to patients. You may also want to know, before or upon hiring, the relevant policies, procedures, and benefits that you will you receive as an employee. You can ask current employees and/or check the company's website, where you may find their set of core values.

Check out your local library as well. Libraries often provide a wealth of untapped information and opportunities. For example, they may have literacy centers where people can study for the GED or learn English as a second language. Not only do libraries have books about career building, but they may provide access to job and grant search engines, newspapers, relevant magazines, as well as resume assistance.

Do not hesitate to ask questions or ask for help. No matter if you are looking for a job or are already in one, no matter if you are brainstorming for business ideas or searching for marketing trends for your existing business, it does not hurt to do your research and ask.

Research who you want to work with – companies, teams, bosses, individuals, clients. Collaboration works wonders for career success. This is not only about team projects and rock bands, and it does not eliminate independence and autonomy either. Interdependence, a term that Stephen Covey elaborates upon in *The 7 Habits of Highly Effective People*, is both an ingredient and a fruit of collaboration.

Asking is one of the first steps toward collaboration. Understand the strengths of the other party while you acknowledge how you can contribute. Listen to what they say, also because they may offer more than what you know. They may also offer less!

If you are running a business and/or working in the field of marketing, you can ask others for feedback on your performance, your products/ services, and your ideas. You can run focus groups, conduct polls on social media, or survey random people. Through research, you can help predict the potential success of an idea and determine what you need to make it a reality.

Also ask for an accountability partner and a mentor. Your accountability partner can help you stay on track with your goals, and you can do the same for him or her. A mentor can coach you and help you use various methods to achieve your goals. A mentor may only be adept in certain fields, so research can be helpful to determine where and from whom you need guidance. For example, if you know someone successful in public speaking, you may reach out to ask questions, take his/her course(s), watch his/her speeches, and/or read his/her books.

YouTube star Lilly Singh went through depression and made her humorous videos to overcome this issue. Building her career while rising to fame, she has received mentorship from some celebrities. One of them is wrestler/actor, Dwayne "The Rock" Johnson, who advised her to take on the responsibility of self-care.

Research opens the door to many opportunities. Keep your eyes, ears, heart, and mind open. With knowledge and the courage to ask, you take two steps forward to career success.

Your Instant Insights...

- Research for career opportunities, your health condition, and your rights and responsibilities.

- Look for evidence-based information.

- Ask questions and reach out for help.

Getting Accommodations

Sometimes, you might feel like a bother if you ask.

But when they are your needs, speak up.

If you have a disability, you can get accommodations for an exam, an interview, and even on-the-job responsibilities and events. If you are deaf, for example, you can get an American Sign Language interpreter.

"Someone has to stand up and speak for the freedoms of the little guy," politician Christopher Monckton said.

Sometimes, we all might feel like the "little guy" or the minority. But that "someone to stand up and speak" needs to be you and me, since we know ourselves well. If you are reading this, you have the power of self-advocacy.

You do not need to have a disability to need accommodations. For example, your workplace might have an ergonomics program that assesses your office needs according to how comfortable, safe, and healthful your working conditions are. Experts check to see if your chair and computer monitor are too high or too low. They may recommend ways to improve your sitting and standing position, such as getting a cushion for the seat or a foot rest so your feet do not dangle.

If you feel sick or if you have appointments, there may be times when you need to take an hour or a day off.

If you are not well, you will be less productive and have less presence of mind, or mindfulness, at work.

Here is a modern inspirational story about speaking up for your needs.

Madalyn Parker, a web developer, emailed her team and her company's CEO to ask for two days off due to mental health reasons. The CEO, Ben Congleton, sent his reply: he thanked her for notifying them, for reminding them that mental health is also as important as physical health, and for raising awareness to reduce stigma. This became sensational, viral news, with many people praising Congleton and even expressing hopes to work at his company. He later posted online, discussing how mental health is still – yet should not be – controversial in the workplace.

Not only did Congleton show a great example as a great leader, but he paves the way for opportunity for those living with mental and/or (other) chronic health conditions.

So do not be afraid to ask.

As Parker did, champion yourself and form a network of champions. Not only did she champion her cause at her company, but she spread her message around the world via social media. You can do the same.

For example, if you have diabetes, it may be helpful to educate at least one person in your office about what to do in case of an emergency (recognizing the signs and symptoms, the proper use of a glucometer, and the administration of insulin as needed).

If you experienced a stroke, you can educate others on recognizing what a stroke looks like.

Educate others. Also reach out to your workplace and community resources.

If your workplace has a wellness program, why not participate and take the opportunities offered?

Remember: your life and your health matter, and you are a priority. Your contributions matter, but you would perform best when you are well. So when you help yourself, know you are not alone.

Break the stigma. Bring others with you along your journey.

Your Instant Insights...

- Do not be afraid to ask for accommodations.

- Champion yourself and build a network of champions.

- Be resourceful and be a resource – educate.

Worsening Health

Sometimes, you fear work will worsen your health.

If you effectively manage your time, stress, and health, and if you enjoy and love your work, the fear may go away. Your health may stay the same or even get better.

Research has shown that unemployment can lead to many health problems and a higher risk of death. Unemployment causes stress and affects psychological health as well.

However, as the publisher Michael Forbes said, "Presence is more than just being there."

Presenteeism – where you are present physically at work but not mindfully – is common. This affects the quantity and quality of performance, reducing productivity, which is a wasteful cost for employers. According to the Harvard Business Review, every year, presenteeism costs the United States more than $150 billion. This includes presenteeism due to depression ($35 billion a year) and pain conditions ($47 billion a year).

You matter. Your health matters. Your presence and your presence of mind matter. Your time and your performance matters.

One of the best ways to recuperate after work is to sleep. You might consider taking power naps as well. Sleep re-charges and refreshes you, and good sleep practices are a must. Two tips are to sleep between 7-8 hours per day and to go to bed at a relatively early hour.

Currently, two sleep philosophies of leaders and entrepreneurs exist. One message is *work hard, long hours until you reach your goal*. The other, supported by the likes of Michael Hyatt and Arianna Huffington, is *sleep does not hinder but can help you toward success*.

We are humans. We need sleep.

Do not neglect yourself while at work, after work, and before work.

At work, join a wellness program if one exists. If it does not, advocate for one. A wellness program involves various aspects. One of these can be occupational health – safety of the environment and different requirements of the job, such as lifting, carrying, or pushing and pulling. Another can be nutrition and/or physical activity. For example, yoga classes can be offered during lunch break, and the cafeteria or vending machines can offer healthy food options.

Wellness programs are cost-effective to employers because these programs help take care of employees, who are assets to the company.

Time management is a third key.

I love doing checklists either at the beginning or end of my workday, and I love seeing progress with those check marks. Sometimes, I make them on sticky notes; other times, I use a small dry-erase board.

If I get stuck on one project or await its approval, I look at my checklist and proceed to work on another. This may sound like multi-tasking, but this still involves focusing mindfully on one task at a time.

I also often use the calendar on my phone for scheduling plans and appointments. Though I juggle many projects, I aim for a healthy workload. I may delegate certain tasks or work with a team sometimes. Nevertheless, I aim to do the best I can.

During weekends and vacations, I may travel, with a mix of business, leisure, and faith. I visit churches and pray not only for my health, but for the recovery of many others who are sick. I attend self-development courses. I go sightseeing and see friends too.

You can spend your free time to relax and indulge in a hobby. You can explore your creativity.

The late professor, author, and speaker, Randy Pausch suffered from cancer. His popular recorded lectures on video covered subjects such as time management, fulfilling dreams, and living life to the fullest. He believed in leaving a powerful legacy and thus, despite his wife's initial hesitation, he gave the world "The Last Lecture." In this speech, he even did push-ups to demonstrate that he was "okay."

Pausch showed purposefulness in life. Through his accomplishments, he enriched the lives of millions, beyond his students and his family. He was mindful in his work. He loved life despite terminal illness.

So love your life and live your life no matter the circumstances. Let your work give you fulfillment, and let your service benefit others. Let it be a circle of joy.

Loving and living life also means taking care of your health and taking the time to enjoy yourself.

No perfect life exists, yet even imperfections make life perfectly beautiful. Live your story...a story true to you.

Your Instant Insights...

- Have enough sleep every day.

- Join or start a wellness program at work.

- Manage your time wisely.

Losing Productivity

Break down your goals into stepping-stones.

Have you ever feared you would not be productive at work because of your health?

Zig Ziglar, an inspirational author and speaker said, "You were born to win, but to be a winner, you must plan to win, prepare to win, and expect to win."

Victory is not only for those with perfect health. It can also be claimed by people living with chronic conditions. The same may be said about productivity.

Productivity, like success, can be self-defined. Is it the number of tasks you accomplished for the day? Or is it the milestones you made in a year?

A sense of fulfillment can arise from productivity, no matter the amount of time.

If you would like to be a prolific writer but have difficulty writing, typing, or sitting for long hours, why not try this? First outline your book. Then record your content verbally into a digital voice recorder. Finally, have the recording transcribed (perhaps by rev.com) and the transcript edited.

You may, like me, not always feel comfortable recording your voice. Yet, I feel I need to do my research, and I find some pleasure in typing or handwriting. Therefore, I define productivity in writing by the number of words and/or chapters finished.

Defining your terms of productivity can help reduce stress. Many entrepreneurs, such as some video instructors and coaches, emphasize the "hustle." However, to take care of your own health, define your own terms of "hustle," and aim to work smart. For example, your guidelines might include getting enough sleep at night, taking stretching or walking breaks, and using automated or simplified processes. Simplification can involve employing customizable templates – ranging from emails to fliers – instead of making them from scratch.

Manage not only your stress, but also your health. If you need to take medications, stick to a daily regimen. Keep your medical appointments. Watch for your signs and symptoms. You may also ask someone close to you, such as family members or a best friend, to look out for you as well.

If you are new in your job, find support from someone within your department or company. You can also shadow people to learn more about your role. For example, when I was teaching, I shadowed professors in two different colleges and took note of what made their styles effective. You can also get a mentor or job coach. I have even heard of a company that offers a dream coach!

However, you should also heed the advice of Shark Tank billionaire entrepreneur, Robert Herjavec, who said "Stop the 'Will you by my mentor?' emails and start being present to embrace the learning opportunities all around you."

For example, you may ask advice from your boss.

Also, financial advisor Suze Orman said that the best mentors do not force you to copy them, but they allow you to become your best self.

Support can come from the Employee Assistance Program, if your company has one. One service you may avail is the mental health therapy, where you can talk about your triumphs, problems, and anything else on your mind.

Be purposeful in your breaks. Sometimes, we take them to talk to someone on the phone, or more often, to check social media. You can take breaks to re-energize yourself: a mini-power nap, a healthy snack, a stretch, a walk, a few minutes of meditation, something to keep you healthy and re-focused later.

Most of all, don't forget to celebrate each accomplishment, big or small, each workday. Take each night to reflect with gratitude on what made you joyful that day. Otherwise, you can use the few minutes before you get out of bed to make a mental gratitude list of at least three items. Hopefully, one item on the list will celebrate how productive you were yesterday.

Another way to celebrate and to encourage celebrations is to create an employee celebrations board at work or a personal board at home. For the company setting, this can be an icebreaker or a teambuilding exercise. Posts on employee celebration boards might include new additions to the family (babies or pets), successful work events, and great customer satisfaction rates/testimonials.

You may throw a little party or potluck at work. It may be for a birthday, a random holiday, to celebrate something big, or just "because we are a cool team." Consider celebrating female colleagues on International Women's Day or during Women's History Month.

Richard Branson, the billionaire behind the Virgin brand, grew up with dyslexia. His teachers in school did not recognize or accommodate his condition. Yet he accepted his learning disability, learned more about it, and uses it to his advantage in areas that range from management to negotiation to delegation.

Branson's parents and his uncle were among the biggest influencers in his life. His uncle lived his own advice: do not conform and be free even to do what everyone calls "crazy." Branson experienced many moments when he did not follow everyone's opinion, but decided the opposite for himself and succeeded.

Everyone has a different story, and so do you. It is important to know and acknowledge yourself and your needs. In your uniqueness, define your own terms of productivity and success. You need not overwhelm yourself with everyone's advice. Do what feels right and true to you.

Remember to take meaningful pauses and to celebrate your blessings. Be grateful, and expect that the best is yet to come.

Your Instant Insights...

- Manage your stress and health condition. Define your terms of productivity.

- Get a mentor/coach and job support.

- Take purposeful breaks and celebrations.

Handling Stress

Be whole, and live a wholehearted life.

These are keys to managing stress.

Have you ever been overwhelmed by a huge workload or a complicated project? If you are seeking a job, do certain application processes daunt you? Do you feel that you are on the verge of not making it: missing the deadline, feeling angry or frustrated, or getting sick? Do you take too long to wake up or repeatedly hit the snooze button in the morning?

You may need a healthy balance.

Being whole and living wholeheartedly is healthy. Dr. Bill Hettler, co-founder of the National Wellness Institute, developed the Six Dimensions of Wellness model. These dimensions are occupational, physical, social, intellectual, emotional, and spiritual. All these are needed for balance in life.

For occupational wellness, your work needs to align with your values, skills, and interests. Work satisfaction is important, and engagement is key.

Physical wellness means taking care of your body through positive habits and elimination of negative habits. This begins by living in a healthy environment. Regular exercise and good nutrition are also important and help relieve stress. The internal chemicals for happiness and energy are released in our nervous system when we exercise and eat healthy food.

Social wellness involves contributing to our community/environment unselfishly and harmoniously. Realizing your positive impact on others and your environment can make your day great. It is also good to interact with other people – not only on social media – to improve in personal communication skills, to develop self-esteem, and to not isolate yourself often in a bubble.

Research has shown that altruism, which involves generosity and kindness, has a direct relationship with happiness. This means that if you do kind things to others in a day, you will be happy. Plus, the happier you become due to past generosity – from yourself and/or others – you feel more motivated to do more kind things.

So take time to be kind. You can take it as a challenge. At the end of the day, can you list three acts of generosity or kind words you have shared with others?

Intellectual wellness is about expanding your mind through creativity, problem-solving, and learning. Avoid procrastination, which can prolong or worsen your anxiety. Challenge yourself to learn something new and to apply the lessons. Read – not only social media – but more of helpful articles and books. You can join or start a book club or a reading challenge at work.

Emotional wellness is when you expect good things to come, and when you become aware and accepting of your feelings. This helps with building and maintaining relationships. This dimension also allows you to face challenges in life and persevere. You understand your capabilities and weaknesses, become more independent, and manage stress effectively.

Spiritual wellness involves living with integrity (being true to ourselves), with meaning and with purpose. It can mean being at peace with yourself first. Cultivating this dimension can involve prayer and meditation, journaling, traveling in nature, and reading Scriptures and inspirational materials.

Though not clearly indicated in the six dimensions of wellness, take care of your financial health too. Develop a habit of saving, at least.

Even during times of hardships, aim to count your blessings. For example, in my life, I saw my chronic condition as an opportunity to express myself creatively through writing and music. Touching other people's lives, I teach them and let them shine too. If I had not let go of my old dream, I would have been more stressed and I would not have explored more of my creative side.

Find occasions to express gratitude, verbally or in silent prayer. Find blessings to be grateful about.

Lizzie Velasquez is a motivational speaker born with a genetic disorder that prevents her from gaining weight and affects her eyes, heart, and bones. She was bullied since kindergarten and cyber-bullied during her teen years because of her appearance. A cruel video about her changed her life. From then on, she decided she would speak up for herself, and in turn become a voice for others, including bullying victims. She is now a successful speaker and author.

To the person who labeled her "the ugliest woman in the world," she posted an online letter of thanks. She also said, "Awful things happened to me, but I am still here smiling and happy. I am so grateful that what I have been through has given me the opportunity to be a voice for so many people."

Velasquez lives with passion and her message is full of integrity.

Accept who you are, the blessings you receive, and the dimensions of wellness you now have. Even if you feel you lack in one dimension or so, it is never too late to change. Invest in yourself and your well-being. Invest in your values.

Your Instant Insights...

- Cultivate all the dimensions of wellness in your life.

- Take time to share kindness with others.

- Find the silver lining even during stressful times, and be grateful.

Workplace Bullies

Bullying is negative, and it hurts.

Have you suffered bullying at work, perhaps due to a health condition?

Though I did not disclose my health condition, I once suffered bullying in a former workplace too. This damaged my self-esteem, which hampered my performance.

Bullying may come from supervisors, colleagues, clients, or students.

Bullying may be verbal, such as using offensive language/tone or threats against you. It can also be in written form. It may be physical harassment. It may be psychological and occupational such as making you do (inappropriate) tasks beyond your scope of work or excluding you from important meetings.

If this occurs to you, you can document the incident and you may choose to speak to the bully with diplomacy. You can report it to your manager and/or human resources department, especially if this repeats on multiple occasions. When you document, be accurate and recall who else witnessed the incident(s).

Like Richard Branson, you can take handwritten notes often. It has helped him during legal cases for example.

If the workplace bullying or harassment is severe, especially if it worsens your health and/or productivity, get an advocate. This can be a conflict and resolution specialist, an ADA specialist, a lawyer, a union, and so on.

In Denver, Colorado, a supermarket employee became subject to bullying because of his learning disability. Two store supervisors harassed and teased him repeatedly. Eventually, he was terminated after working at the supermarket for a decade. With the law on the bullied man's side, the supermarket chain was sued and had to pay $80,000 in settlement.

Remember: someone cares for you, and you are not alone. When you know others may feel alone in their hardship, you can be their voice as well as yours.

Take the opportunities to stand, be yourself, and speak up for your rights. You do not need to be an extrovert to do this. You can write, speak one-on-one or in groups, or express yourself in other ways.

Bullying is the bully's way of expressing his/her personal insecurities, as many anti-bullying advocates say.

However, bullying is never okay, and neither is passing down insecurity.

Trust in the Golden Rule. You may pray for and/or forgive your bullies. However, remedy the situation before it is too late.

You have a voice. Use it to tell the truth. As Jesus said, "The truth will set you free." (John 8:32 -NIV)

You have power – the power to make a difference, the power to set a light, the power to become free.

You have a conscience. Use your wisdom and power for positive change.

You have a heart. Let no one abuse your ability to live and speak from the heart.

You have a soul. Enrich it with your work and the joy work can give. Bring your soul relief when restorative, social justice – not necessarily revenge – comes. Calm your soul with faith, hope, and compassion.

You have eyes and ears. Be a witness to righteousness, and help others who need help.

You have a mind. It is not about minding your own business only, but reminding yourself and others that your business is to serve.

To those who are served, be thankful for others and how they serve you, from your teachers who stay up late at night grading papers to the farmworkers who harvest crops in the summer heat.

We all have the power to serve. We all need the power of love. We all hold the opportunity to express gratitude.

Your Instant Insights...

- Document and report.

- Get an advocate.

- Stand and speak up for yourself.

Loving Your Work

Love your work.

Physicist/cosmologist Stephen Hawking said, "Work gives you meaning and purpose, and life is empty without it."

Yet have you ever dreamt of an ideal job or business? Does your current job drain your energy? Can you truthfully say, "I love my job"?

Two philosophies exist about work and passion:

1. Do the work you love.
2. Love the work you do.

These philosophies can be combined. You can do the work you love by finding a job or business that fits you and is true to your ideals. You can love the work you do by learning more and falling in love with the mission and the process. Involve all your skills and talents. Ask how you can contribute to the job's overall goal.

You can love your work environment too, especially if it has a supportive, friendly culture.

When looking for a job or business, delve deep into self-discovery. What do you need and want? What can you do? What work activities give you joy?

Research next. Read the job descriptions and listen to yourself. Picture yourself in that position. If some aspects of the job are not suitable or appropriate for you, do not be afraid to say no. But if the job description still sounds good and you do not have some of the required skills, aim to learn them either before you apply or as on-the-job training.

For example, I earned my Certified Worksite Wellness Specialist credential from the National Wellness Institute to supplement my educational background and training as a health education specialist. My employer also offers classes in CPR and Microsoft Office. I have taken the opportunity to learn more in-depth skills in Excel and Word.

Therefore, while in your job or running a business, do not be afraid to learn. You can attend events with guest speakers who can show you different aspects of work, from laws to data security and more. If you cannot attend them in person, try webinars or virtual attendance.

Another way of loving your work more is to cultivate a positive work environment. Be friendly to your workmates. Smile when you speak, and speak with a positive tone. You do not need to always disclose or complain about your health.

Remember: you represent your work or business. It is important to love who/what you represent. This makes you look more reliable, trustworthy, and likeable.

This is not about being a 100% people-pleaser. But passion is contagious. Your good attitude can lead to more happy customers and coworkers. A pleasant environment can then make you happy in return.

Believe in the mission and values of your company. See the good in them. Strive to incorporate at least one of these values into your work and life. For example, if continuous improvement is one of your company's core values, why not strive for this on a personal level – read motivational books, watch motivational talks, practice and improve your craft?

When you love your work, you will be happier and healthier. At least, you will thrive in the occupational, spiritual, intellectual, and emotional dimensions of wellness.

You can use your chronic condition as a focal point of your passion and work. After becoming paralyzed due to an accident, former *Superman* actor Christopher Reeve founded the Christopher Reeve Paralysis Foundation, which promotes research into spinal cord injuries. He set a good example of speaking up by talking to a Senate subcommittee to promote stem cell research. His paralysis also did not stop him from making more movies.

Reeve said, "Once you choose hope, anything's possible."

Among superheroes, we often look at physical strength, such as that of Superman and Wonder Woman. However, why not look at the mental powers of Professor X as well? And why not see we all have superhero potential, no matter the condition we face?

Our work, done with heart and with our best, can make a big impact. Superheroes do great work, and so can we. Superheroes are unique, and so are we.

We do not always need to hide, whether with a mask, a hood, or paint.

The superhero in us is waiting. The superhero is not our physical, mental, or emotional condition. And these qualities are not the domain of the super villain either.

The superhero is both the worker and the boss within ourselves.

Go. Be your own superhero.

Your Instant Insights...

- Dig into self-discovery and research when looking for a job or business.

- Cultivate a positive work environment.

- Work according to the mission and core values of your company. Fall in love with the super work you do and the superhero you have become.

About the Author

Diana Hallare spent her childhood as a Filipina expatriate in the Middle East. She moved to California when she was a teenager.

Today, Diana is a multicultural community health advocate, public speaker, and Certified Worksite Wellness Specialist with a Master's degree in Public Health from the University of Manchester, England. Her work experiences include organizing art shows for people living with disabilities, facilitating creative writing groups, teaching both college and high school students, and promoting breastfeeding and chronic disease prevention/management. She understands chronic conditions not only from a scientific or public health perspective, but also from a personal point of view.

Her mission: the empowerment of diverse people to become champions for their wellbeing and to live with joy as they fulfill their potential.

Connect with the Author

Website:
www.chroniconomics.com

Email:
chroniconomics@gmail.com

Social Media:
Facebook:
fb.me/dianahallare.author

LinkedIn:
https://www.linkedin.com/in/dianahallare/

Acknowledgements

To my family – for your love and support in my endeavors

To Joy Marie Hallare and Colleen Battistoni – for your work on my website

To my father – for providing inspiration and advice on entrepreneurship

To Crescendo Publishing, including Robbin Simons and Shayna Rohrig – for helping me fulfill my publishing dream

To Clarene M. White – for being a good friend and mentor who introduced me to social entrepreneurship

To Dr. Aimee V. Sanchez and Elda Dorothy – for being among my cheerleaders

To the Arts Consortium – for allowing me a space to share my creative works

To the local government/nonprofit/ university programs and community resources – for the opportunity to thrive with meaningful work

To other friends who stood by my side

To those who helped save my life

Thank you

Resources

Groups /Events
Toastmasters International: Leadership and
Communication (www.toastmasters.org)
Abilities Expo (www.abilities.com)
American Association of People with Disabilities
(www.aapd.com)

Grassroots Movements
Walk with a Doc
National Alliance on Mental Illness

Mentors
Journey of the Heart Ministries: for women
facing struggles (www.journeyoftheheart.org)
Micromentor: for entrepreneurs in progress
(www.micromentor.org)

A Micro List of Health-Related Nonprofits
Alzheimer's Association (www.alz.org)
American Cancer Society (www.cancer.org)
American Diabetes Association (www.diabetes.
org)
American Heart Association (www.heart.org)
American Stroke Association (www.
strokeassociation.org)

Websites

ReWork: social innovation for meaningful work (www.rework.jobs)
Idealist: meaningful work including jobs and internships (www.idealist.org)
Bender Consulting: recruiting people with disabilities (www.benderconsult.com)
Health Talk Online: Patient experiences (www.healthtalk.org)

Books

Your Life Without Limits by Nick Vujicic

References

Altucher, James. "Ultimate Guide for Becoming an Idea Machine." **http://www.jamesaltucher. com/2014/05/the-ultimate-guide-for-becoming-an-idea-machine/**

Biography.com. "Christopher Reeve." **https://www.biography.com/people/ christopher-reeve-9454130**

Bureau of Labor Statistics. (June 21, 2017). "Persons with a Disability: Labor Force Characteristics Summary." **https://www.bls.gov/news.release/ disabl.nr0.htm**

Calfas, Jennifer. (June 11, 2017). "Meet the CEO Whose Comments about Mental Health in the Workplace Went Viral." *Time.* **http://time.com/money/4853305/ mental-health-workplace-olark-madalyn-parker-ben-congleton/**

CBS News. (December 2, 2016). "Cookie orders roll in at business owned by woman with Down syndrome." **http://www.cbsnews.com/news/ cookie-orders-roll-in-business-owned-by-woman-with-down-syndrome/**

Charles, Jeff. (April 27, 2016). "A Sleeping Entrepreneur Is a Successful Entrepreneur." *Huffington Post.* **http://www.huffingtonpost.com/ jeff-charles/a-sleeping-entrepreneur-i_b_9787272.html**

Cox, Jessica. **http://www.rightfooted.com**

Dixon, Alex. (September 6, 2011). "Kindness Makes You Happy... and Happiness Makes You Kind." *Greater Good Magazine.* **https://greatergood.berkeley.edu/ article/item/kindness_makes_you_ happy_and_happiness_makes_you_kind**

Entis, Laura. "5 Famous Business Leaders on the Power of Mentorship." *Entrepreneur.* **https://www.entrepreneur.com/ slideshow/249233**

Haas, Mariah. (July 25, 2015). "Lilly Singh on Struggling with Depression: 'It's Nothing to Be Ashamed About." *People.* **http:// people.com/celebrity/lilly-singh-on-struggling-with-depression-its-nothing-to-be-ashamed-about/**

Hemp, Paul. (October 2004). "Presenteeism: At Work – But Out of It." *Harvard Business Review.*

https://hbr.org/2004/10/
presenteeism-at-work-but-out-of-it

Holberton School.
http://www.holbertonschool.com

James, Susan Donaldson. (August 31, 2015).
"Lizzie Velasquez: 'Ugliest woman' video
changed my life for the better." *Today*.
http://www.today.com/health/lizzie-
velasquez-ugliest-woman-video-
changed-my-life-better-t41361

Kluger, Jeffrey. (Sept. 12, 2014). "FDR's Polio: The
Steel in His Soul." *Time*.
http://time.com/3340831/polio-fdr-
roosevelt-burns/

Leahy, Robert. (February 5, 2013).
"Unemployment Is Bad for Your Health."
Huffington Post.
http://www.huffingtonpost.com/
robert-leahy-phd/unemployment-
health_b_2616430.html

Mission U.
http://www.missionu.com

Morin, Amy. (April 3, 2015). "7 Scientifically
Proven Benefits of Gratitude." *Psychology
Today*.
https://www.psychologytoday.com/
blog/what-mentally-strong-people-

dont-do/201504/7-scientifically-proven-benefits-gratitude

National Wellness Institute. "The Six Dimensions of Wellness Model." http://www.nationalwellness.org/?page=Six_Dimensions

Neithercott, Tracey. (July 2012). "Cliff Scherb: Ironman Athlete with Type 1." *Diabetes Forecast.* http://www.diabetesforecast.org/2012/jul/cliff-scherb-ironman-athlete-with-type-1.html

New International Version Bible. https://www.thenivbible.com/

Pausch, Randy. (September 18, 2007). "Last Lecture: Achieving Your Childhood Dreams." https://www.youtube.com/watch?v=ji5_MqicxSo

Pausch, Randy. (November 2007). "Time Management." https://www.youtube.com/watch?v=oTugjssqOT0

Schwartz, Emily. (November 7, 2012). "Richard Branson and the dyslexia advantage." *The Washington Post.* https://www.washingtonpost.com/national/on-innovations/

richard-branson-and-the-dyslexia-advantage/2012/11/07/67a05b2a-2906-11e2-bab2-eda299503684_story.html?utm_term=.a66497d8dc8c

Steinberg, Jacob. (Sept. 13, 2016). "Kadeena Cox: I wanted to show it can be done even if you have setbacks." *The Guardian.* **https://www.theguardian.com/sport/2016/sep/13/kadeena-cox-rio-paralympics-gold**

Texas Council for Developmental Disabilities. (October 20, 2015). "Workplace Bullying: Know Your Rights." **http://www.tcdd.texas.gov/workplace-bullying/**

U.S. Equal Employment Opportunity Commission. (December 13, 2011). "King Soopers to Pay $80,000 to Settle EEOC Disability Discrimination Lawsuit." **https://www.eeoc.gov/eeoc/newsroom/release/12-13-11.cfm**

Velasquez, Lizzie. (September 22, 2015). "To the Person Who Called Me 'the World's Ugliest Woman' in a Viral Video." *The Mighty.* **https://themighty.com/2015/09/lizzie-velasquez-response-to-worlds-ugliest-woman-video/**

Vrajlal, Alicia. (September 10, 2015). "No wonder she's called Superwoman!" *Daily Mail.* **http://www.dailymail.co.uk/tvshowbiz/article-3229013/IISuperwomanII-star-Lilly-Singh-reveals-valuable-advice-Rock-given-s-like-kissing-Seth-Rogen-ahead-Sydney-s-Youtube-Fan-Fest.html**

Vujicic, Nick. **http://www.lifewithoutlimbs.org**

About Crescendo Publishing

Crescendo Publishing is a boutique-style, concierge VIP publishing company assisting entrepreneurs with writing, publishing, and promoting their books for the purposes of lead-generation and achieving global platform growth, then monetizing it for even more income opportunities.

Check out some of our latest best-selling AuthorPreneurs at
http://CrescendoPublishing.com/new-authors

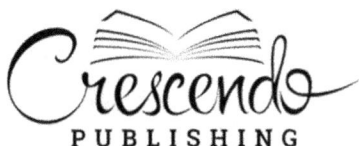

Crescendo
PUBLISHING

About the Instant Insights™ Book Series

The *Instant Insights™ Book Series* is a fact-only, short-read, book series written by EXPERTS in very specialized categories. These high-value, high-quality books can be produced in ONLY 6-8 weeks, from concept to launch, in BOTH PRINT & eBOOK Formats!

This book series is FOR YOU if:

- You are an expert in your niche or area of specialty

- You want to write a book to position yourself as an expert

- You want YOUR OWN book – NOT a chapter in someone else's book

- You want to have a book to give to people when you're speaking at events or simply networking

- You want to have it available quickly

- You don't have the time to invest in writing a 200-page full book

- You don't have a ton of money to invest in the production of a full book – editing, cover design, interior layout, best-seller promotion

- You don't have a ton of time to invest in finding quality contractors for the production of your book – editing, cover design, interior layout, best-seller promotion

For more information on how you can become an *Instant Insights™* author, visit **www.InstantInsightsBooks.com**

More Books in the
Instant Insight Series

A Time Management System *for* Creative Entrepreneurs	Branding & Website Essentials *for* Entrepreneurs	How to Create & Build a Successful Beauty Business	Organizing Your Workspace *for* a Productivity Boost
How to be a Happy & Prosperous CEO	Taking Your Business from Start Up to Thrive in 45 Days	7 Strategies *for* Raising Calm, Inspired, & Successful Children	Creating a Solid, Lasting Connection with Your Kids
12 Leadership Powers *for* Successful Women	Motivation: Your Master Key to Success & Riches!	Performance Power: Clarity, Confidence & Joy	Practical Natural Healing Tips *for* Vibrant Living
The Art of Selling to a Woman	Unconventional Methods *for* Writing a Best Selling Book	Defining Moments with Family, Friends, & More	Building a Conflict-Proof Relationship

Crescendo

CrescendoPublishing.com